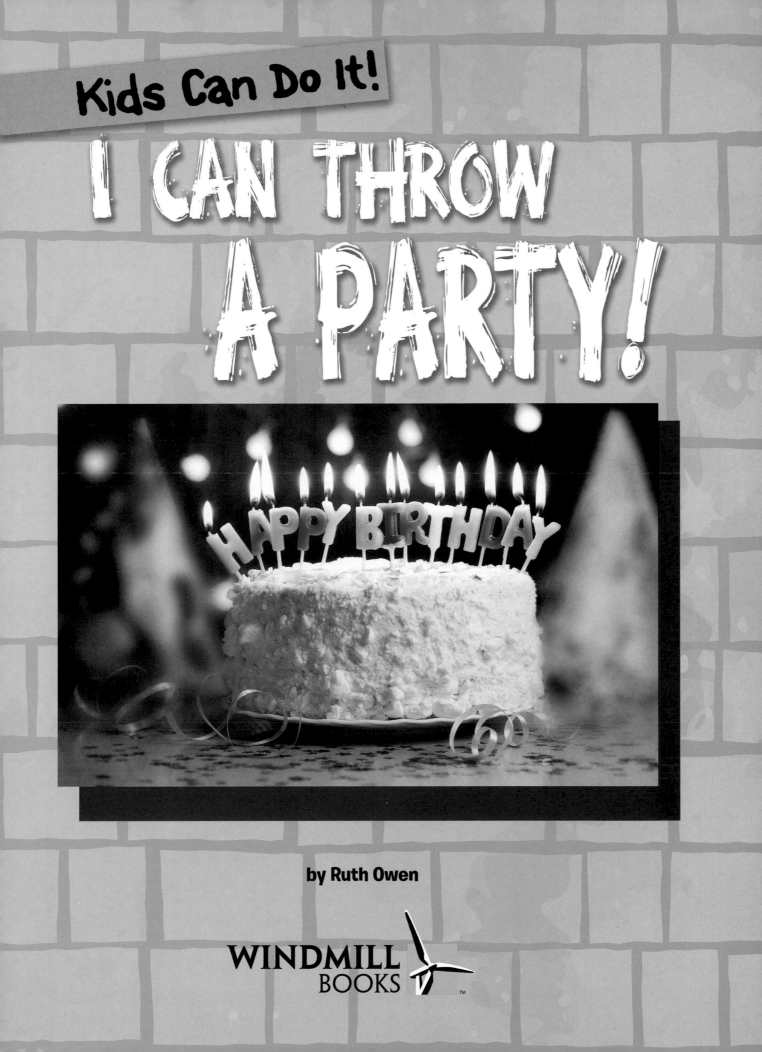

Kids Can Do It!

I CAN THROW A PARTY!

by Ruth Owen

WINDMILL
BOOKS

Published in 2018 by **Windmill Books**, an Imprint of Rosen Publishing
29 East 21st Street, New York, NY 10010

Produced for Rosen by Ruby Tuesday Books Ltd
Designer: Tammy West

Photo Credits: Courtesy of Ruby Tuesday Books and Shutterstock.

Cataloging-in-Publication Data
Names: Owen, Ruth.
Title: I can throw a party! / Ruth Owen.
Description: New York : Windmill Books, 2018. | Series: Kids can do it! | Includes index.
Identifiers: ISBN 9781499483550 (pbk.) | ISBN 9781499483499 (library bound) |
   ISBN 9781499483383 (6 pack)
Subjects: LCSH: Children's parties--Juvenile literature. | Parties--Planning--Juvenile literature. |
   Entertaining--Juvenile literature.
Classification: LCC GV1205.094 2018 | DDC 793.2'1--dc23

Manufactured in the United States of America
CPSIA Compliance Information: Batch BS17WM: For Further Information contact Rosen Publishing, New York, New York at 1-800-237-9932

WARNING:

Some of the activities in this book require adult help.
The author and publisher disclaim any liability in connection
with the use of the information in this book.

CONTENTS

COME TO A PARTY!

Whether Halloween is just around the corner, or your birthday is coming up, it's always a good time to throw a party!

Once you've got permission to throw a party and the date is set, what needs to happen next? To be a successful **host**, you'll need to organize invitations, decorations, food, and games.

Inside this book, you'll find some great ideas that will help your party stand out from the crowd — without costing a fortune!

So get planning and creating . . .
. . . and let's throw a party!

When should you send out invitations? There's no rules about this, but about four weeks before the party will usually be enough time to make sure everyone saves the date.

POPSICLE INVITATIONS

These cute, colorful, popsicle-themed invitations are made using recycled paint swatches.

You will need:
- Tracing paper
- A pencil
- Scissors
- Paint swatches
- White printer paper
- A computer
- Glue
- Popsicle sticks
- Ribbon

1 Begin by tracing the popsicle shape on tracing paper. Cut out the shape.

2 To make each invitation, use the paper template to cut out two popsicle shapes from a paint swatch.

3 Glue the two halves of the invitation together with a popsicle stick sandwiched between the two.

4 On a computer, create the text for the invitation and print it out on white paper. Trim the text to the desired size and glue it to one side of the popsicle.

5 Finally, glue a small bow to the front of the popsicle stick.

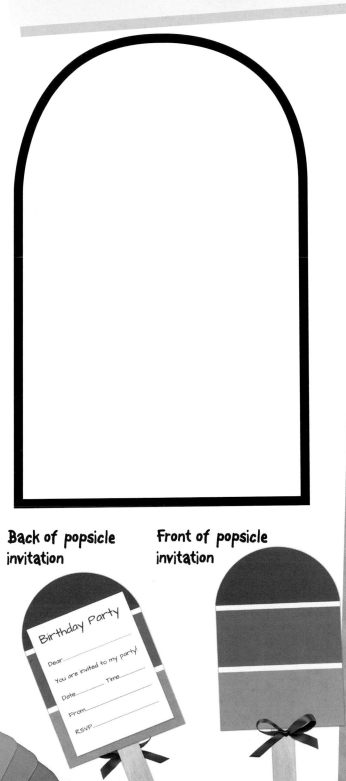

Back of popsicle invitation

Birthday Party
Dear
You are invited to my party!
Date _____ Time _____
From
RSVP

Front of popsicle invitation

HALLOWEEN PARTY INVITATIONS

You will need:

- Tracing paper
- A pencil
- Scissors
- Thin black card stock
- White, silver, or gold pencils or pens
- Paper fasteners

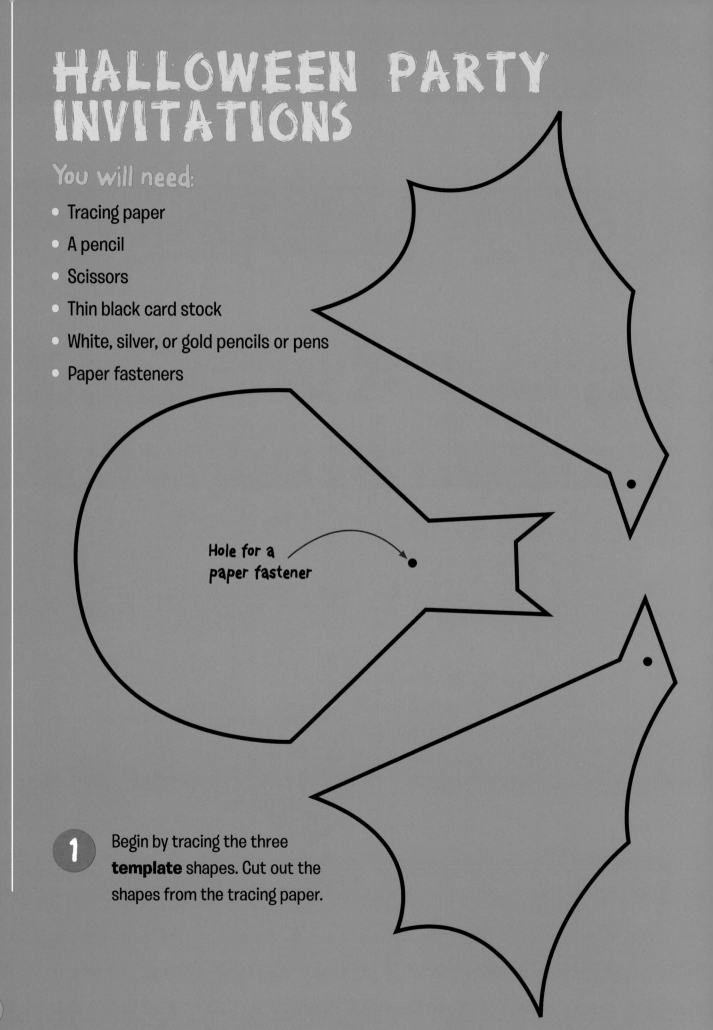

Hole for a paper fastener

1 Begin by tracing the three **template** shapes. Cut out the shapes from the tracing paper.

2 To make one invitation, lay the three paper shapes on the black card stock. Use a white pencil or pen to draw around the shapes, and then cut them out.

3 Mark the spot on each shape where the hole should be. Carefully pierce a small hole in each shape using the point of the scissors.

4 Position the three pieces of card stock so their holes are overlapping. Push a paper fastener through the holes. Next, bend and flatten the two legs of the paper fastener to secure the pieces of card stock together.

Take care when using the scissors to cut the paper and card stock, and when piercing the holes.

Paper fastener

5 The wings of the bat will now open to reveal the body section underneath. Using a white, gold, or silver pen, write your invitation.

6 Close up the bat's wings, and your Halloween invitations are ready to send or hand out to your friends.

You are invited to a
Halloween Party!
Clare and David's House
October 31st
6:00 pm to 9:00 pm

MAKE PARTY BUNTING

Strings of decorative bunting can be hung indoors and outdoors. Bunting looks festive and can be made in your favorite colors, or personalized to fit any party theme.

You will need:

- Craft paper, cardboard, or felt
- Scrap cardboard
- A pencil
- Scissors
- A hole punch
- Thin ribbon, string, or yarn
- Glue

1 To make paper bunting, begin by making a triangle template. Draw a triangle in the size you want on a piece of scrap cardboard and cut it out.

Cardboard template

2 Place the template on your colored paper, lightly draw around the template with a pencil, and then cut it out.

You can make bunting in your favorite colors.

Try making bunting in your team's colors.

3 For a superhero-themed party, photocopy pages from comics and magazines. You can even recycle old comics and cut your bunting triangles directly from a comic's pages.

4 Use a hole punch to punch two holes in each triangle.

Holes

5 Thread ribbon, string, or yarn through the holes, as shown. When the bunting is the desired length, tie a knot in each end to keep the triangles in place.

If you're having a Halloween party, try making bunting that features some favorite spooky characters, such as Dracula, Frankenstein's monster, a ghost, and a jack-o'-lantern.

You can make fantastic Halloween faces from felt or crafting foam.

1 To make a face, place a cardboard template on a piece of felt or foam. Draw around the template with a pencil, and then cut it out.

Felt

Foam

The ribbon will go through here.

2 Fold over the top edge of the triangle and glue down to form a narrow hem, or tube. The ribbon or string of the bunting will go through this hem.

3 Now the fun part begins! Create a Halloween face on the triangle by gluing on small pieces of felt.

Old buttons can also be used to create the eyes and other features of your Halloween faces.

4 When the faces are all complete, string them onto a length of ribbon, string, or yarn.

THROW A PIZZA PARTY

Almost everyone loves pizza, which makes it a great party food!

On the morning of your party, prepare homemade pizza bases and tomato sauce. Then when it's time to eat at your party, get your guests to build their own individual pizzas.

The ingredients on this page will be enough to make 8 small pizzas.

Ingredients:

For the pizza base:
- 6 cups strong white flour
- 2 teaspoons salt
- 0.5 ounce packet of easy bake yeast
- 4 tablespoons olive oil
- 2 cups of warm water
- Flour for dusting
- Oil for greasing baking pans

For the tomato sauce:
- 2 onions
- 4 garlic cloves
- 2 tablespoons olive oil
- 1 teaspoon salt
- 2 cans (14 ounces) chopped tomatoes
- 4 heaped teaspoons tomato puree
- 1 teaspoon sugar
- 2 tablespoons dried basil
- 2 lemons
- 1 teaspoon black pepper
- Ready-grated mozzarella cheese
- Your choice of topping ingredients

Equipment:

- Sieve
- Mixing bowl
- Cutting board
- Plastic wrap
- Knife
- Garlic crusher
- Saucepan
- Wooden spoon
- Paper towels
- A small pizza baking pan for each guest
- Rolling pin
- Bowls and spoons
- Pizza cutter

1. Sift the flour and salt into a mixing bowl.

2. Add the yeast, olive oil, and water to the bowl.

Easy bake yeast

3. Mix the ingredients into a ball of **dough** with your hands.

4. Sprinkle some flour onto a cutting board. Place the ball of dough onto the board and start **kneading**. Push, squeeze, and pull the dough for about eight minutes, until it's smooth and springy.

Kneading the dough

5. Place the dough back into the mixing bowl. Cover the bowl with plastic wrap and place it in a warm place for an hour, or until it's doubled in size.

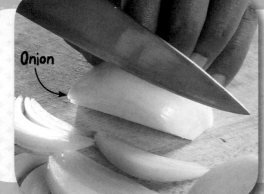

Onion

IT'S ALL ABOUT TEAMWORK

When using a knife, the stove, or an oven, always make sure an adult is helping you.

6 To make the tomato sauce, chop the onions into small pieces and crush the garlic cloves.

Crushed garlic

Garlic clove

7 Pour the olive oil into a pan and heat over a medium heat.

Soft, cooked onions

8 Add the chopped onions and half the salt to the pan. Gently cook the onions until they are soft (about 5 minutes). Add the crushed garlic.

9 Add the tomatoes, tomato puree, sugar, basil, a big squeeze of lemon juice, and the remaining salt and pepper to the pan.

Dried basil

10 Stir the sauce and leave it to gently bubble for about 10 minutes. Put in a sealed container and store in a refrigerator.

Tomato puree

11 Use a paper towel to smear a little olive oil over the baking pans. This will keep the pizzas from sticking to the pans.

12 Once the pizza dough has risen, place it on a flour-dusted board again and knead for about one minute. Divide the dough into eight pieces.

13 Use a rolling pin or your hands to flatten the dough. Place the pizza bases on the oiled baking pans.

14 On a large table or kitchen countertop, set out bowls of different pizza toppings, grated mozzarella, and a big bowl of your homemade tomato sauce.

15 When it's time to eat, preheat the oven to 450 °F (230 °C).

16 Give each guest a pizza base on a baking tray and tell them to help themselves to tomato sauce, cheese, and other toppings.

Make sure you supply plenty of spoons for serving the pizza toppings, and napkins for cleaning up spills!

 17 Bake the pizzas for 15 to 20 minutes. While you're having fun making pizzas with your friends, ask an adult to be in charge of putting the pizzas into the oven and taking them out once they're baked.

Have a competition to discover who can create the best pizza design!

FRESH FRUIT POPSICLES

At a summer party, WOW your guests with colorful, homemade fresh fruit popsicles.

You will need:

- Your choice of berries and other fruit
- A knife and cutting board
- Popsicle molds
- Apple juice
- Wooden popsicle sticks

1 Wash your selection of berries and other fruits. Peel your fruit if needed, and slice or chop larger fruits into small pieces or thin slices.

IT'S ALL ABOUT TEAMWORK

Make sure an adult is close by when you're using a knife.

2 Pack the popsicle **molds** with fruit. If the fruit is pressed against the sides of the molds, the popsicles will look better.

3 Pour apple juice into each mold. Don't fill completely to the top of the mold, as the juice will expand as it freezes.

4 Carefully push a wooden popsicle stick into each mold.

When it's time to eat the popsicles, you can quickly run them under hot water to help free them from the molds.

5 Put the popsicles into a freezer overnight, and then enjoy!

MAKE A DELICIOUS ICE CREAM BUFFET

Create an exciting dessert for your party guests with this fun project.

A **buffet** is a selection of foods from which people serve themselves. Your guests will love creating and eating a delicious range of ice cream sundaes and cones!

1 To create an ice cream buffet, cover a table with a white or colorful tablecloth. You can set up a buffet indoors or outdoors.

2 Set out small bowls of sprinkles, candy, nuts, chocolate chips, and chopped fruit. There are no rules! Be inventive and give your guests lots of choices.

Put a spoon in each bowl for sprinkling the treats onto the ice cream.

Give your guests a choice of syrups to pour over their ice cream, too.

3 Place cones and small bowls with spoons on the buffet table.

4 Finally, when your guests are ready to eat dessert, place a large container of vanilla ice cream on the table with an ice cream scooper.

5 Tell your guests that the buffet is open and it's time to have fun making and eating ice cream treats!

MAKE A PIÑATA

Have fun with your party guests playing a piñata game. You can buy piñatas in many different shapes, or get creative and make your own.

The shell of this homemade piñata is made of **paper-mache.** All you need to make paper-mache is some white glue and old newspapers.

You will need:

You will need:

- A balloon
- Two pieces of string approximately 8 feet (2 m) long
- A plastic ziplock bag
- Newspapers
- White glue (mixed three parts glue to one part water)
- A paintbrush
- Colorful recycled paper scraps
- Wrapped candy

Make your piñata in advance of your party. You will need at least five days to make the piñata and allow it to dry.

1 Blow up the balloon so it's about 14 inches (35 cm) long.

2 Tie the two pieces of string to the knot of the balloon. Tie each string in its center so you end up with four long strands of string hanging from the balloon.

Put the strings into the plastic bag to protect them from the glue.

3 Tear about six sheets of newspaper into strips that are 1 inch (3 cm) wide. Torn edges make a better paper-mache surface than cut edges.

4 Brush some of the glue mixture onto the side of the balloon with a paintbrush. Lay a strip of newspaper onto the glue, and then brush more glue over the top.

5 Continue adding more newspaper strips, slightly overlapping each strip. Cover the balloon, but leave a small area uncovered at the top. Let the paper-mache dry for 24 hours.

6 Bring the four strings up the side of the balloon and knot them above the hole in the paper-mache.

7 Add a second layer of paper strips, covering the strings. Place the strips in a different direction than the first layer. Allow the newspaper to dry for 24 hours.

8 Apply a third and then a fourth layer of paper-mache, allowing each layer to dry for 24 hours.

9 When the paper-mache is dry, decorate it with scraps of paper. You can use wrapping paper, tissue paper, and even shapes cut from magazine pages.

You can cut your paper into squares, rectangles, petal shapes, or even hearts.

Pop the balloon through the hole and remove it.

 Fill the piñata with candy, and then plug the hole with more tissue paper.

 The piñata is now ready to hang up and smash!

PARTY GAMES: ZOMBIE AUTOPSY

If you're throwing a Halloween party or a zombie-themed birthday party, this funny, gross, and horrifying game will have your guests screaming and laughing!

To play the game, your guests will need to touch wobbly, squishy, and yucky bits of a zombie's body as they take part in a zombie **autopsy**. In reality, they'll be touching some carefully chosen foods.

You will need:

- 8 small cardboard boxes
- A craft knife
- 8 bowls
- Foods to make zombie body parts
- Paper and pencils

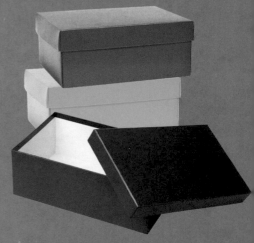

Always make sure an adult is close by when using a craft knife.

1 To set up the game, take eight small cardboard boxes. Shoe boxes are perfect for this activity because they have lids.

Cut a small hole in the box's lid.

2 Using a craft knife, carefully cut a small hole in the lid of each box. The hole should be just big enough to fit a person's hand.

3 Place a bowl containing one of your foods inside each box.

4 Line up the boxes on a table or countertop. Label the boxes 1 to 8.

Zombie Body Part Number 1

FOODS FOR ZOMBIE BODY PARTS

Here are some ways that you can make zombie body parts using food. Have fun thinking up your own ideas, too.

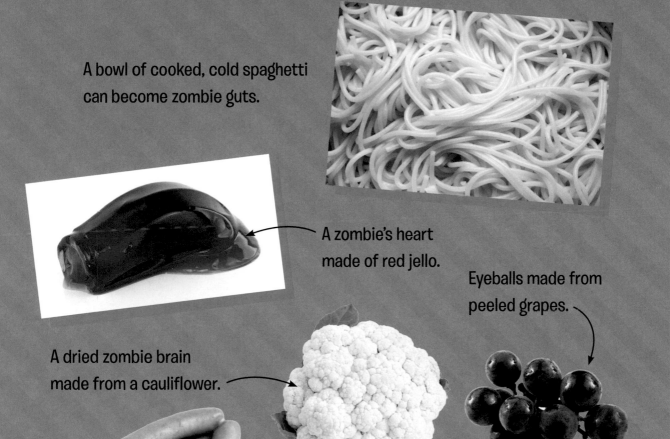

A bowl of cooked, cold spaghetti can become zombie guts.

A zombie's heart made of red jello.

Eyeballs made from peeled grapes.

A dried zombie brain made from a cauliflower.

Lumps of beef jerky will feel like crusty flakes of zombie skin.

Zombie fingers made from hot dogs.

Rotting zombie teeth made of popcorn.

A lumpy pickle can become a zombie's nose.

HOW TO PLAY ZOMBIE AUTOPSY

When your guests are ready to play, introduce the game with a gruesome story.

1 Tell your guests they are the survivors of a **zombie apocalypse**. Today, they must help examine the **dissected** body of a zombie.

Welcome to the Zombie Autopsy

A severed hand
Halloween decoration

2 In turn, each player puts their hand into the eight boxes to feel the body parts. The player must guess which body part is in the box. The player then writes down their guess on an answer sheet.

BOX NUMBER	ZOMBIE BODY PART	WHAT KIND OF FOOD?
1		
2		
3		
4		
5		
6		
7		
8		

3 Each player must also guess what the body part is really made of.

4 The winner of the game is the player who gets the most guesses correct.

Your guests may feel bold when they first start playing. However, once they see their friends screaming and recoiling from the boxes' yucky contents, some players may not be brave enough to try every box!

GLOSSARY

autopsy
A detailed examination of a dead body.

buffet
A meal that includes lots of different dishes from which guests serve themselves.

dissected
Cut into pieces to be scientifically studied.

dough
A thick mixture of flour and other ingredients, including liquids such as water or milk, used for making baked goods such as bread, pizza, and cookies. Dough is firm and can be formed into shapes.

host
A person who throws and arranges an event such as a party.

kneading
To blend ingredients together to form dough, by squeezing, pushing, and pulling, using hands or a food processor.

molds
Hollow containers that are used to give shape to a liquid once it has frozen, or to a hot liquid substance once it has cooled and hardened.

paper-mache
A material made from newspapers and glue that can be molded when it is wet. Paper-mache hardens as it dries, so it can be used for making models and sculptures.

template
A shaped piece of material, such as cardboard, that is used as a pattern for cutting out.

zombie apocalypse
A fictional global event in which zombies (the undead) rise up and try to do harm to the living.

WEBSITES

For web resources related to the subject of this book, go to:
www.windmillbooks.com/weblinks and select this book's title.

INDEX